Jemima Blackburn

Bible Beasts and Birds

A new edition of illustrations of scripture by an animal painter

Jemima Blackburn

Bible Beasts and Birds
A new edition of illustrations of scripture by an animal painter

ISBN/EAN: 9783337309770

Printed in Europe, USA, Canada, Australia, Japan

Cover: Foto ©Andreas Hilbeck / pixelio.de

More available books at **www.hansebooks.com**

BIBLE BEASTS
AND BIRDS

A NEW EDITION

OF

ILLUSTRATIONS OF SCRIPTURE BY
AN ANIMAL PAINTER

BY

MRS. HUGH BLACKBURN

PHOTOGRAPHED FROM THE ORIGINALS
AND PRINTED IN PLATINOTYPE

LONDON
KEGAN PAUL, TRENCH & CO., 1, PATERNOSTER SQUARE
1886

ADVERTISEMENT.

At the end of the year 1854, Messrs. Constable of Edinburgh published a series of twenty Photographs from Drawings by Mrs. Hugh Blackburn, under the title "Illustrations of Scripture by an Animal Painter, with Notes by a Naturalist."

Sir Edwin Landseer wrote to the publishers of that work : "If any praise of mine can add to the popularity of this charming work, I have great pleasure in repeating my sincere admiration for its extreme originality of conception and admirable accuracy of knowledge of the creatures delineated. Having studied animals during my whole life, perhaps my testimony as to the truth of the artist's treatment of the Scripture Illustrations may have some influence."

Mr. Thackeray and Mr. Ruskin also wrote letters which it is pardonable to reproduce, though they have already been printed in "English Female Artists, by Ellen C. Clayton."

"36 Onslow Sq^r. Brompton.—
16 Feb. (1855).

"Dear Mrs. Blackburn,

"Two days since, Millais and Phillips Portrait-painter and Leech were dining with me and the Scripture Animals were on the table.

"These gentlemen said the drawings were the finest they had seen for ever so long a time ; and two of them went off with an intention of buying the book straightway—sure the best compliment that artists can pay a sister artist.

v

"Now is the time, thinks I, to write that note to Mrs. Blackburn— Mrs. HUGH Blackburn, which you owe her this ever so long a time—even she, living in a cloister, surrounded by the grave and wise, will not be displeased at hearing by what critics her genius is appreciated. The pictures grow upon me like all good things. I spy out little secrets unperceived before—why, it was not till last night I saw the little beak of the chick under the hen peering out from the beautiful fluffy white maternal feathers. I dont know whether I like that or the Owls or the Deluge or the Scape-goat best—I think the Swine running into the sea is a grand composition ; and the Plague of Frogs—well, I must own that the plague of frogs made me laugh—especially that fellow jumping into the vase. The pretty little Egyptian ballet-children are very quaint and pleasant to look at—and guorrawarrawow how those dogs are serving Jezebel right ! Those vultures coming up are very fine and tragic. What a deal of pleasure you have given me !

"The Times dined with me yesterday, and I urged upon him the necessity of enlightening the public respecting these drawings.

"Not that I suppose the public will really care for them, and the dreadful fee of two guineas will operate as a barrier between you and popularity. I know I wouldn't sell *my* copy for two guineas, though I got it at a considerable reduction ! That cost of production * was one of the questions I was going to ask you when I got the book first—a query answered by your note and the price put on the book.

"I have been to Paris twice since I owed you this note—to visit my parents—to be ill—to fetch home my daughters—have had a very great deal to write and to do,—otherwise I should have written earlier to thank you for the great pleasure which you have given me and continue to give me. That boy must have the love of animals and the sportsman instinct strongly developed in him, to make such a remark as that about Jezebel's paint. I hope I shall know him some day and see more drawings in your portfolio.

---

* To those curious, like Thackeray, as to the "cost of production," it may be interesting to learn that the artist's share of the profits of this publication was some copies presented to friends.

"Give my best regards to Lushington and to Thomson please with his nice wife; and pardon me for forgetting your husband's Xtian name. U and I (a neat and novel pun) are very different—you can draw and have worked and have done it. I ought to have could, and have been idle, and neglected that good gift. I always feel sad and ashamed when I think of this.

"Ever yours, dear Mrs. Blackburn,

"Very sincerely,

"W. M. THACKERAY."

"DEAR MRS. BLACKBURN,

"I have your book and am much pleased with it. It is impressive and in many respects delightfully original. I like Jezebel better than I expected—only she needn't have had quite such a broad foot,—and I like Pharaoh—frowning at the sea—and I like the little girl who don't like Frogs, and I like Lazarus, (perhaps the best of all), and I like the ape talking to the peacock about his tail, and I like intensely the swallow and stork. But how in the world could you poke the best beloved Ass into the stall with the ox? Of all the beasts she should have been first —you should have put her with her colt at the meeting of the two ways. And how in the world could you miss the *Serpent?*

"Bill with his sticks is delightful. I had not caught the idea of the crown of thorns. I wish you had written the illustrations yourself—you know the printer would have put the spelling to rights.

"I *cannot* get you inventive people to explain your own notions in a plain way to the public.

"I am writing something about the book. Would you ask your publisher—No—I'll manage it myself.

"Ever faithfully yours,

"J. RUSKIN."

This work was perhaps the first ever published with photographic illustrations. The art of photography was then little understood, and

vii

hardly practised commercially; the prints were "silver" prints—consequently perishable—and most of the copies, in the course of thirty years, have practically perished.

Now that there are several photographic processes which are *permanent*, Mrs. Blackburn has been urged by friends, interested in art, to republish her drawings, and she has ventured on the present *Edition de Luxe.* The Platinotype process has been selected, both for its artistic merits and as giving results which will last unaltered as long as the paper on which they are printed. The plates are on a scale one-half larger than those of the former issue.

Of the twenty drawings in the former issue two have been rejected as inferior ; one of these is the Ox and the Ass referred to by Mr. Ruskin. Four new drawings have been introduced ; these are "The Firstborn of Egypt," "The Fowls of the Air," "The Viper," and the "Horses and Ships." The Notes by a Naturalist have not been reprinted, and the letterpress consists solely of extracts from the Bible, and illustrative quotations from Milton, for which last the reprint by Pickering of the Text of the *Editio Princeps* of the "Paradise Lost" of 1667 has been used, as giving as nearly as may be Milton's own idea of spelling and emphasis.

The plates have been executed by Mr. William Mansfield of St. Mary Cray, Kent, and will speak for themselves to connoisseurs ; they are φωνᾶντα συνετοῖσι.

LIST OF PLATES.

BIBLE BEASTS
AND BIRDS.

I.

THE RAVEN.

AND it came to pass at the end of forty days, that Noah opened the window
of the Ark which he had made :

And he sent forth a Raven, which went forth to and fro, until the Waters
were dried up from off the Earth.

Also he sent forth a Dove from him, to see if the Waters were abated from
off the face of the ground ;

But the Dove found no rest for the sole of her foot, and she returned unto
him into the Ark ; for the Waters were on the face of the whole Earth :

Then he put forth his hand, and took her, and pulled her in unto him
into the Ark.

And he stayed yet other seven days ; and again he sent forth the Dove
out of the Ark :

And the Dove came in to him in the evening ; and, Lo, in her mouth was
an Olive leaf pluckt off :

So Noah knew that the Waters were abated from off the Earth.

And he stayed yet other seven days ; and sent forth the Dove ; which
returned not again unto him any more.

GENESIS VIII. 6-12.

1   B

But the Dove found no rest for the sole of her foot
and she returned unto him unto the Ark

II.

THE DOVE.

ALSO he sent forth a Dove from him, to see if the Waters were abated from
off the face of the ground ;

But the Dove found no rest for the sole of her foot, and she returned unto
him into the Ark ; for the Waters were on the face of the whole Earth :

Then he put forth his hand, and took her, and pulled her in unto him into
the Ark.

And he stayed yet other seven days ; and again he sent forth the Dove
out of the Ark :

And the Dove came in to him in the evening ; and, Lo, in her mouth was
an Olive leaf pluckt off :

So Noah knew that the Waters were abated from off the Earth.

And he stayed yet other seven days ; and sent forth the Dove ; which
returned not again unto him any more.

GENESIS VIII. 8-12.

> "He look'd, and saw the Ark hull on the floud,
> Which now abated, for the Clouds were fled,
> Driv'n by a keen North-winde, that blowing drie
> Wrinkl'd the face of Deluge, as decai'd ;
> And the cleer Sun on his wide watrie Glass
> Gaz'd hot, and of the fresh Wave largely drew,
> As after thirst, which made thir flowing shrink
> From standing lake to tripping ebbe, that stole
> With soft foot towards the deep, who now had stopt
> His Sluces, as the Heav'n his windows shut.
> The Ark no more now flots, but seems on ground
> Fast on the top of som high mountain fixt.

THE DOVE.

And now the tops of Hills as Rocks appeer ;
With clamor thence the rapid Currents drive
Towards the retreating Sea thir furious tyde.
Forthwith from out the Arke a Raven flies,
And after him, the surer messenger,
A Dove sent forth once and agen to spie
Green tree or ground whereon his foot may light ;
The second time returning, in his Bill
An Olive leafe he brings, pacific signe :
Anon drie ground appeers, and from his Arke
The ancient Sire descends with all his Train."

Paradise Lost, Ed. 1067, bk. x. ll. 836–858.

Abraham said — My Son, God will provide himself a lamb for a burnt-offering

JB

III.

THE RAM CAUGHT IN THE THICKET.

AND it came to pass after these things that GOD did tempt Abraham, and
said unto him, Abraham : and he said, Behold, here I am.

And He said, Take now thy Son, thine only son Isaac, whom thou lovest,
and get thee into the land of Moriah ; and offer him there for a burnt
offering upon one of the mountains which I will tell thee of.

And Abraham rose up early in the morning, and saddled his ass, and took
two of his young men with him, and Isaac his Son, and clave the wood
for the burnt offering, and rose up, and went unto the place of which
GOD had told him.

Then on the third day Abraham lifted up his eyes, and saw the place
afar off.

And Abraham said unto his young men, Abide ye here with the ass ; and
I and the Lad will go yonder and worship, and come again to you.

And Abraham took the wood of the burnt offering, and laid it upon Isaac
his Son ; and he took the fire in his hand, and a knife ; and they went
both of them together.

And Isaac spake unto Abraham his Father, and said, My Father : and he
said, Here am I, my Son.   And he said, Behold the fire and the wood :
but where is the Lamb for a burnt offering ?

And Abraham said, My Son, GOD will provide Himself a Lamb for a burnt
offering:

So they went both of them together.

And they came to the place which GOD had told him of; and Abraham built an Altar there, and laid the wood in order, and bound Isaac his Son, and laid him on the Altar upon the wood.

And Abraham stretched forth his hand, and took the knife to slay his Son.

And the Angel of the LORD called unto him out of Heaven, and said, Abraham, Abraham :

And he said, Here am I.

And He said, Lay not thine hand upon the Lad, neither do thou anything unto him : for now I know that thou fearest GOD, seeing thou hast not withheld thy Son, thine only Son from me.

And Abraham lifted up his eyes and looked, and, Behold, behind him a Ram caught in a thicket by his horns ; and Abraham went and took the Ram, and offered him up for a burnt offering in the stead of his Son.

GENESIS XXII. 1–13.

By faith Abraham, when he was tried, offered up Isaac : and he that had received the promises offered up his only begotten Son, of whom it was said, That in Isaac shall thy seed be called :

Accounting that GOD was able to raise him up even from the dead ; from whence also he received him in a figure.

HEBREWS XI. 17–19.

IV

THE PLAGUE OF FROGS.

AND the LORD spake unto Moses, Go unto Pharaoh, and say unto him, Thus saith the LORD, Let My people go, that they may serve Me.

And if thou refuse to let them go, Behold, I will smite all thy borders with Frogs :

And the River shall bring forth Frogs abundantly, which shall go up and come into thine House, and into thy Bedchamber, and upon thy Bed, and into the House of thy Servants, and upon thy People, and into thy Ovens, and into thy Kneading Troughs :

And the Frogs shall come up both on thee, and upon thy people, and upon all thy servants.

And the LORD spake unto Moses, Say unto Aaron, Stretch forth thine hand with thy rod over the Streams, over the Rivers, and over the Ponds, and cause Frogs to come up upon the Land of Egypt.

And Aaron stretched out his hand over the Waters of Egypt; and the Frogs came up, and covered the Land of Egypt.

And the Magicians did so with their enchantments, and brought up Frogs upon the Land of Egypt.

Then Pharaoh called for Moses and Aaron, and said, Entreat the LORD, that He may take away the Frogs from me, and from my people; and I will let the People go, that they may do sacrifice unto the LORD.

And Moses said unto Pharaoh, Glory over me: when shall I entreat for thee, and for thy servants, and for thy people, to destroy the Frogs from thee and thy houses, that they may remain in the River only ?

And he said, To-morrow.   And he said, Be it according to thy word; that thou mayest know that there is none like unto the LORD our GOD.

And the Frogs shall depart from thee, and from thy houses, and from thy servants, and from thy people; they shall remain in the River only.

And Moses and Aaron went out from Pharaoh : and Moses cried unto the LORD because of the Frogs which He had brought against Pharaoh.

And the LORD did according to the word of Moses; and the Frogs died out of the Houses, out of the Villages, and out of the Fields.

And they gathered them together upon heaps; and the Land stank.

But when Pharaoh saw that there was respite, he hardened his heart, and hearkened not unto them ; as the LORD had said.

EXODUS VIII. 1–15.

> " But first the lawless Tyrant, who denies
> To know thir God, or message to regard,
> Must be compelld by Signes and Judgements dire;
> To blood unshed the Rivers must be turnd,
> Frogs, Lice and Flies must all his Palace fill
> With loath'd intrusion, and fill all the land."
>
> *Paradise Lost*, Ed. 1667, bk. x. ll. 1064–1069.

And all the first born in the land of Egypt shall die -

V

THE FIRSTBORN.

AND Moses said, Thus saith the LORD, About midnight will I go out into the midst of Egypt :

And all the Firstborn in the Land of Egypt shall die, from the Firstborn of Pharaoh that sitteth upon his Throne, even unto the Firstborn of the Maidservant that is behind the mill ; and all the Firstborn of Beasts.

And there shall be a great cry throughout all the Land of Egypt, such as there was none like it, nor shall be like it any more.

And it came to pass, that at midnight the LORD smote all the Firstborn in the Land of Egypt, from the Firstborn of Pharaoh that sat on his Throne, unto the Firstborn of the Captive that was in the Dungeon ; and all the Firstborn of Cattle.

And Pharaoh rose up in the night, he, and all his servants, and all the Egyptians ; and there was a great cry in Egypt ; for there was not a House where there was not one dead.

EXODUS XI. 4–6 ; XII. 29, 30.

The Horse and his rider hath He thrown into the Sea

VI

THE HORSE AND HIS RIDER.

AND it was told the King of Egypt that the People fled: and the heart of
Pharaoh and of his servants was turned against the People, and they
said,

Why have we done this, that we have let Israel go from serving us?

And he made ready his Chariot, and took his people with him:

And he took six hundred chosen Chariots, and all the Chariots of Egypt,
and Captains over every one of them.

And the LORD hardened the heart of Pharaoh King of Egypt, and he
pursued after the Children of Israel: and the Children of Israel went
out with an high hand.

But the Egyptians pursued after them, all the Horses and Chariots of
Pharaoh, and his Horsemen, and his Army, and overtook them
encamping by the Sea, beside Pi-hahiroth, before Baal-zephon.

And when Pharaoh drew nigh, the Children of Israel lifted up their eyes,
and, Behold, the Egyptians marched after them; and they were sore
afraid: and the Children of Israel cried out unto the LORD.

And they said unto Moses, Because there were no graves in Egypt, hast
thou taken us away to die in the Wilderness? Wherefore hast thou
dealt thus with us, to carry us forth out of Egypt?

Is not this the word that we did tell thee in Egypt, saying, Let us alone,
that we may serve the Egyptians? For it had been better for us to
serve the Egyptians, than that we should die in the Wilderness.

And Moses said unto the People, Fear ye not, stand still, and see the Salvation of the LORD, which He will shew to you to-day: For the Egyptians whom ye have seen to-day, ye shall see them again no more for ever.

The LORD shall fight for you, and ye shall hold your peace.

And the LORD said unto Moses, Wherefore criest thou unto Me? Speak unto the Children of Israel, that they go forward :

But lift thou up thy Rod, and stretch out thine hand over the Sea, and divide it: and the Children of Israel shall go on Dry ground through the midst of the Sea.

And I, Behold, I will harden the hearts of the Egyptians, and they shall follow them : and I will get Me honour upon Pharaoh, and upon all his Host, upon his Chariots, and upon his Horsemen. And the Egyptians shall know that I am the LORD, when I have gotten Me honour upon Pharaoh, upon his Chariots, and upon his Horsemen.

And the Angel of GOD, which went before the Camp of Israel, removed and went behind them ; and the Pillar of the Cloud went from before their face, and stood behind them. And it came between the Camp of the Egyptians and the Camp of Israel ; and it was a Cloud and Darkness to them, but it gave Light by night to these : so that the one came not near the other all the night.

And Moses stretched out his hand over the Sea ; and the LORD caused the Sea to go back by a strong East wind all that night, and made the Sea Dry land, and the Waters were divided.

And the Children of Israel went into the midst of the Sea upon the Dry ground : and the Waters were a Wall unto them on their right hand and on their left.

And the Egyptians pursued, and went in after them to the midst of the Sea, even all Pharaoh's Horses, his Chariots, and his Horsemen.

And it came to pass, that in the Morning Watch the LORD looked unto the Host of the Egyptians through the Pillar of Fire and of the Cloud, and troubled the Host of the Egyptians, and took off their Chariot Wheels,

that they drave them heavily : so that the Egyptians said, Let us flee from
the face of Israel ; for the LORD fighteth for them against the Egyptians.

And the LORD said unto Moses, Stretch out thine hand over the Sea, that the
Waters may come again upon the Egyptians, upon their Chariots, and
upon their Horsemen.

And Moses stretched forth his hand over the Sea, and the Sea returned to his
strength when the morning appeared ; and the Egyptians fled against it;

And the LORD overthrew the Egyptians in the midst of the Sea.

And the Waters returned, and covered the Chariots, and the Horsemen,
and all the Host of Pharaoh that came into the Sea after them ; there
remained not so much as one of them.

But the Children of Israel walked upon Dry land in the midst of the Sea ;
and the Waters were a Wall unto them on their right hand, and on
their left.

Thus the LORD saved Israel that day out of the hand of the Egyptians ; and
Israel saw the Egyptians dead upon the Sea shore.

And Israel saw that Great Work which the LORD did upon the Egyptians :

And the People feared the LORD, and believed the LORD, and His servant
Moses.

Then sang Moses and the Children of Israel this song unto the LORD, and
spake, saying,

I will sing unto the LORD, for He hath triumphed gloriously :

The Horse and his Rider hath He thrown into the Sea.

The LORD is my Strength and Song, and He is become my Salvation : He
is my GOD, and I will prepare Him a habitation ; my Father's GOD,
and I will exalt Him.

The LORD is a man of War : The LORD is His name.

Pharaoh's Chariots and his Host hath He cast into the Sea : his chosen
Captains also are drowned in the Red Sea.

The Depths have covered them : they sank into the bottom as a stone.

Thy right hand, O LORD, is become glorious in power : Thy right hand, O
LORD, hath dashed in pieces the Enemy.

And in the Greatness of Thine Excellency Thou hast overthrown them that rose up against Thee : Thou sentest forth Thy Wrath, which consumed them as stubble.

And with the Blast of Thy nostrils the Waters were gathered together, the Floods stood upright as an Heap, and the Depths were congealed in the Heart of the Sea.

The Enemy said, I will pursue, I will overtake, I will divide the Spoil ; my Lust shall be satisfied upon them ; I will draw my Sword, my hand shall destroy them.

Thou didst blow with Thy Wind, the Sea covered them : they sank as lead in the mighty Waters.

Who is like unto Thee, O LORD, among the Gods ? Who is like Thee, glorious in Holiness, fearful in Praises, doing Wonders ?

Thou stretchedst out Thy Right Hand, the Earth swallowed them.

Thou in Thy mercy hast lead forth the People which Thou hast redeemed : Thou hast guided them in Thy Strength unto Thy Holy Habitation.

The People shall hear and be afraid : Sorrow shall take hold on the Inhabitants of Palestina.

Then the Dukes of Edom shall be amazed ; the mighty men of Moab, trembling shall take hold of them : all the Inhabitants of Canaan shall melt away.

Fear and Dread shall fall upon them ; By the Greatness of Thine Arm they shall be as still as a stone : till Thy People pass over, O LORD, till the People pass over, which Thou hast purchased.

Thou shalt bring them in, and plant them in the Mountain of Thine Inheritance, in the Place, O LORD, which Thou hast made for Thee to dwell in ; in the Sanctuary, O LORD, which Thy hands have established.

The LORD shall reign for ever and ever.

For the Horse of Pharaoh went in with his Chariots and with his Horsemen into the Sea, and the LORD brought again the Waters of the Sea upon them ; but the Children of Israel went on Dry land in the midst of the Sea.

And Miriam the Prophetess, the sister of Aaron, took a Timbrel in her hand; and all the Women went out after her with Timbrels and with Dances.

14

And Miriam answered them, Sing ye to the LORD, for He hath triumphed gloriously : the Horse and his Rider hath He thrown into the Sea.

EXODUS XIV. 5-XV. 21.

Some trust in Chariots, and some in Horses: But we will remember the name of the LORD our GOD.

PSALM XX. 7.

" The Red Sea coast, whose waves orethrew
Busiris and his *Memphian* chivalrie,
While with perfidious hatred they pursu'd
The Sojourners of *Goshen,* who beheld
From the safe shore their floating carkases
And broken Chariot Wheels, so thick bestrown
Abject and lost lay these, covering the Flood,
Under amazement of their hideous change."

Paradise Lost, Ed. 1667, bk. i. ll. 306-313.

" Thus with ten wounds
This River-Dragon tam'd at length submits
To let his sojourners depart, and oft
Humbles his stubborn heart, but still as Ice
More hardn'd after thaw, till in his rage
Pursuing whom he late dismissd, the Sea
Swallows him with his Host, but them lets pass
As on drie land between two christal walls,
Aw'd by the rod of *Moses* so to stand
Divided, till his rescu'd gain thir shoar:
Such wondrous power God to his Saint will lend,
Though present in his Angel, who shall goe
Before them in a Cloud, and Pillar of Fire,
By day a Cloud, by night a pillar of Fire,
To guide them in thir journey, and remove
Behinde them, while th' obdurat King pursues :
All night he will pursue, but his approach
Darkness defends between till morning Watch ;
Then through the Firey Pillar and the Cloud
God looking forth will trouble all his Host
And craze thir Chariot wheels: when by command
Moses once more his potent Rod extends
Over the Sea; the Sea his Rod obeys;
On thir imbattelld ranks the Waves return,
And overwhelm thir Warr."

Paradise Lost, Ed. 1667, bk. x. ll. 1082-1106.

VII.

THE SCAPE GOAT.

And Aaron shall cast lots upon the two Goats; one lot for the Lord, and
the other lot for the Scape Goat.

And Aaron shall bring the Goat upon which the Lord's lot fell, and offer
him for a sin offering:

But the Goat, on which the lot fell to be the Scape Goat, shall be presented
alive before the Lord, to make an atonement with him, and to let him
go for a Scape Goat into the Wilderness.

And when he hath made an end of reconciling the Holy Place, and the
Tabernacle of the Congregation, and the Altar, he shall bring the live
Goat:

And Aaron shall lay both his hands upon the head of the live Goat, and
confess over him all the iniquities of the Children of Israel, and all
their transgressions in all their sins, putting them upon the head of
the Goat, and shall send him away by the hand of a fit man into the
Wilderness.

Leviticus xvi. 8–10, 20, 21.

Surely He hath borne our griefs, and carried our sorrows: yet we did esteem
Him stricken, smitten of God, and afflicted.

All we like sheep have gone astray; we have turned every one to his own
way; and the Lord hath laid on Him the iniquity of us all.

Isaiah liii. 4, 6.

And he that let go the Goat for the Scape Goat shall wash his clothes,
and bathe his flesh in water, and afterward come into the Camp.

D

And the Bullock for the sin offering, and the Goat for the sin offering, whose blood was brought in to make atonement in the Holy Place, shall one carry forth without the Camp: and they shall burn in the fire their skins, and their flesh, and their dung.

LEVITICUS XVI. 26, 27.

For the bodies of those beasts, whose blood is brought into the Sanctuary by the High Priest for Sin, are burned without the Camp.

Wherefore Jesus also, that He might sanctify the people with His own blood, suffered without the Gate.

HEBREWS XIII. 11, 12.

"To whom thus *Michael.* Doubt not but that sin
Will reign among them, as of thee begot;
And therefore was Law given them to evince
Thir natural pravitie, by stirring up
Sin against Law to fight; that when they see
Law can discover sin, but not remove,
Save by those shadowic expiations weak,
The bloud of Bulls and Goats, they may conclude
Some bloud more precious must be paid for Man,
Just for unjust, that in such righteousness
To them by Faith imputed, they may finde .
Justification towards God, and peace
Of Conscience, which the Law by Ceremonies
Cannot appease, nor Man the moral part
Perform, and not performing cannot live.
So Law appears imperfet, and but giv'n
With purpose to resign them in full time
Up to a better Cov'nant, disciplin'd
From shadowic Types to Truth, from Flesh to Spirit,
From imposition of strict Laws, to free
Acceptance of large Grace, from servil fear
To filial, works of Law to works of Faith."

Paradise Lost, Ed. 1667, bk. x. ll. 1176–1197.

But the poor man had nothing, save one little ewe-lamb

JB

VIII

THE EWE LAMB.

AND the LORD sent Nathan unto David. And he came unto him, and said unto him,

There were two men in one City; the one Rich, and the other Poor.

The Rich man had exceeding many Flocks and Herds:

But the Poor man had nothing, save one Little Ewe Lamb, which he had bought and nourished up: and it grew up together with him, and with his Children; it did eat of his own meat, and drank of his own cup, and lay in his bosom, and was unto him as a Daughter.

And there came a Traveller unto the Rich man, and he spared to take of his own Flock and of his own Herd, to dress for the wayfaring man that was come unto him; but took the Poor man's Lamb, and dressed it for the man that was come to him.

And David's anger was greatly kindled against the man; and he said to Nathan, As the LORD liveth, the man that hath done this thing shall surely die:

And he shall restore the Lamb fourfold, because he did this thing, and because he had no Pity.

And Nathan said to David, Thou art the man.

2 SAMUEL XII. 1–7.

IX.

GOATS AND CONIES.

Upon the Rocks of the Wild Goats.

1 SAMUEL XXIV. 2.

The High Hills are a refuge for the Wild Goats; and the Rocks for the Conies.

PSALM CIV. 18.

The Conies are but a feeble folk, yet make they their houses in the Rocks.

PROVERBS XXX. 26.

Knowest thou the time when the Wild Goats of the Rock bring forth?

JOB XXXIX. 1.

Apes and Peacocks

X.

APES AND PEACOCKS.

AND all King Solomon's drinking vessels were of Gold, and all the vessels
of the House of the forest of Lebanon were of pure Gold ; none were
of silver : it was nothing accounted of in the days of Solomon.

For the King had at sea a Navy of Tharshish with the Navy of Hiram :

Once in three years came the Navy of Tharshish, bringing Gold, and Silver,
Ivory, and Apes, and Peacocks.

So King Solomon exceeded all the Kings of the Earth for Riches and for
Wisdom.

And all the Earth sought to Solomon, to hear his Wisdom, which GOD had
put in his heart.

And they brought every man his Present, Vessels of Silver, and Vessels of
Gold, and Garments, and Armour, and Spices, Horses, and Mules, a rate
year by year.

And Solomon gathered together Chariots and Horsemen : and he had a
thousand and four hundred Chariots, and twelve thousand Horsemen,
whom he bestowed in the Cities for Chariots, and with the King at
Jerusalem.

And the King made Silver to be in Jerusalem as stones, and Cedars made he
to be as the Sycomore trees that are in the Vale, for abundance.

But King Solomon loved many strange Women (together with the
Daughter of Pharaoh), women of the Moabites, Ammonites, Edomites,
Zidonians, and Hittites; of the Nations concerning which the LORD

23

said unto the Children of Israel, Ye shall not go in to them, neither shall they come in unto you : for surely they will turn away your heart after their gods :

Solomon clave unto these in love. And he had seven hundred Wives, Princesses, and three hundred Concubines : and his Wives turned away his heart.

For it came to pass, when Solomon was old, that his Wives turned away his heart after other gods : and his heart was not perfect with the LORD his God, as was the heart of David his father.

For Solomon went after Ashtoreth the goddess of the Zidonians, and after Milcom the abomination of the Ammonites.

And Solomon did evil in the sight of the LORD, and went not fully after the LORD, as did David his father.

1 KINGS x. 21–27 ; xi. 1–6.

" For those the Race of *Israel* oft forsook
Their living strength, and unfrequented left
His righteous Altar, bowing lowly down
To bestial Gods ; for which their heads as low
Bow'd down in Battel, sunk before the Spear
Of despicable foes. With these in troop
Came *Astoreth*, whom the *Phœnicians* call'd
Astarte, Queen of Heav'n, with crescent Horns ;
To whose bright Image nightly by the Moon
Sidonian Virgins paid their Vows and Songs,
In *Sion* also not unsung, where stood
Her Temple on th' offensive Mountain, built
By that uxorious King, whose heart though large,
Beguil'd by fair Idolatresses, fell
To Idols foul."

Paradise Lost, Ed. 1667, bk. i. ll. 432–446.

" The crested Cock whose clarion sounds
The silent hours, and th' other whose gay Traine
Adorns him, colour'd with the Florid hue
Of Rainbows and Starrie Eyes."

Paradise Lost, Ed. 1667, bk. vii. ll. 443–446.

JB.

In the portion of Jezreel shall Dogs eat the flesh of Jezebel

XI.

JEZEBEL.

AND it came to pass after these things, that Naboth the Jezreelite had a
Vineyard, which was in Jezreel, hard by the Palace of Ahab King
of Samaria.

And Ahab spake unto Naboth, saying, Give me thy Vineyard, that I may
have it for a Garden of Herbs, because it is near unto my House :
and I will give thee for it a better Vineyard than it ; or, if it seem
good to thee, I will give thee the worth of it in money.

And Naboth said to Ahab, The LORD forbid it me, that I should give the
Inheritance of my Fathers unto thee.

And Ahab came into his House heavy and displeased because of the word
which Naboth the Jezreelite had spoken to him : for he had said,
I will not give thee the Inheritance of my Fathers.   And he laid
him down upon his bed, and turned away his face, and would eat
no bread.

But Jezebel his Wife came to him, and said unto him, Why is thy spirit
so sad, that thou eatest no bread ?

And he said unto her, Because I spake unto Naboth the Jezreelite, and
said unto him, Give me thy Vineyard for money ; or else, if it please
thee, I will give thee another Vineyard for it : and he answered,
I will not give thee my Vineyard.

And Jezebel his Wife said unto him, Dost thou now govern the Kingdom
of Israel ?   Arise, and eat bread, and let thine heart be merry : I will
give thee the Vineyard of Naboth the Jezreelite.

So she wrote Letters in Ahab's name, and sealed them with his Seal, and sent the Letters unto the Elders and to the Nobles that were in his City, dwelling with Naboth.

And she wrote in the Letters, saying, Proclaim a Fast, and set Naboth on high among the People : And set two men, sons of Belial, before him, to bear witness against him, saying, Thou didst blaspheme GOD and the King. And then carry him out, and stone him, that he may die.

And the men of his City, even the Elders and the Nobles who were the inhabitants in his City, did as Jezebel had sent unto them, and as it was written in the Letters which she had sent unto them.

They proclaimed a Fast, and set Naboth on high among the People.

And there came in two men, children of Belial, and sat before him : and the men of Belial witnessed against him, even against Naboth, in the presence of the People, saying, Naboth did blaspheme GOD and the King.

Then they carried him forth out of the City, and stoned him with stones, that he died.

Then they sent to Jezebel, saying, Naboth is stoned, and is dead.

And it came to pass, when Jezebel heard that Naboth was stoned, and was dead, that Jezebel said to Ahab, Arise, take possession of the Vineyard of Naboth the Jezreelite, which he refused to give thee for money : for Naboth is not alive, but dead.

And it came to pass, when Ahab heard that Naboth was dead, that Ahab rose up to go down to the Vineyard of Naboth the Jezreelite, to take possession of it.

And the word of the LORD came to Elijah the Tishbite, saying,

Arise, go down to meet Ahab King of Israel, which is in Samaria : Behold, he is in the Vineyard of Naboth, whither he is gone down to possess it.

And thou shalt speak unto him, saying, Thus saith the LORD, Hast thou killed and also taken possession ? And thou shalt speak unto him, saying, Thus saith the Lord, In the place where Dogs licked the Blood of Naboth shall Dogs lick thy Blood, even thine.

And Ahab said to Elijah, Hast thou found me, O mine Enemy ? And he
answered, I have found thee : because thou hast sold thyself to work evil
in the sight of the LORD.

Behold, I will bring evil upon thee, and will take away thy Posterity.

And of Jezebel also spake the LORD, saying, The Dogs shall eat Jezebel by
the Wall of Jezreel.

Him that dieth of Ahab in the City the Dogs shall eat : and him that dieth
in the Field shall the Fowls of the Air eat.

    *   *   *   *   *   *

And the King of Israel said unto his servants, Know ye that Ramoth in
Gilead is ours, and we be still, and take it not out of the hand of the
King of Syria ?

And he said to Jehoshaphat King of Judah, Wilt thou go with me to
battle to Ramoth-Gilead ? And Jehoshaphat said to the King of
Israel, I am as thou art, my People as thy People, my Horses as thy
Horses.

So the King of Israel and Jehoshaphat the King of Judah went up to
Ramoth-Gilead.

And the King of Israel disguised himself, and went into the Battle.

And a certain man drew a bow at a venture, and smote the King of Israel
between the joints of the harness : wherefore he said unto the driver of
his Chariot, Turn thine hand, and carry me out of the Host ; for I am
wounded.

And the Battle increased that day : and the King was stayed up in his
Chariot against the Syrians, and died at even : and the Blood ran out of
the wound into the midst of the Chariot.

And there went a Proclamation throughout the Host about the going down
of the Sun, saying, Every man to his City, and every man to his own
Country.

So the King died, and was brought to Samaria ; and they buried the King in
Samaria.

And one washed the Chariot in the Pool of Samaria; and the Dogs licked up his Blood; and they washed his Armour; according unto the word of the LORD which He spake.

So Ahab slept with his fathers; and Ahaziah his son reigned in his stead.

And Ahaziah fell down through a lattice in his upper chamber that was in Samaria.

So he died, and Joram son of Ahab reigned in his stead, because he had no son.

And Joram the son of Ahab made war against Hazael King of Syria, in Ramoth-Gilead; and the Syrians wounded Joram.

And King Joram went back to be healed in Jezreel of the wounds which the Syrians had given him at Ramah, when he fought against Hazael King of Syria.

And Elisha the Prophet called one of the Children of the Prophets, and said unto him, Gird up thy loins and take this Box of Oil in thine hand, and go to Ramoth-Gilead : And when thou comest thither, look out there Jehu the son of Jehoshaphat the son of Nimshi, and go in, and make him arise up from among his brethren, and carry him to an inner chamber; Then take the Box of Oil, and pour it on his head, and say, Thus saith the LORD, I have anointed thee King over Israel. Then open the door, and flee, and tarry not.

So the young man, even the young man the Prophet, went to Ramoth-Gilead.

And when he came, Behold, the Captains of the Host were sitting; and he said, I have an errand to thee, O Captain. And Jehu said, Unto which of all of us? And he said, To thee, O Captain.

And he arose, and went into the house; and he poured the Oil on his head, and said unto him, Thus saith the LORD GOD of Israel, I have anointed thee King over the People of the LORD, even over Israel.

And thou shalt smite the House of Ahab thy master, that I may avenge the Blood of My servants the Prophets, and the Blood of all the servants of the LORD, at the hand of Jezebel.

28

For the whole House of Ahab shall perish.

And the Dogs shall eat Jezebel in the Portion of Jezreel, and there shall be none to bury her.

And he opened the door, and fled.

Then Jehu came forth to the Servants of his Lord : and one said unto him, Is all well ? Wherefore came this mad fellow to thee ? And he said unto them, Ye know the man, and his communication.

And they said, It is false ; tell us now. And he said, Thus and thus spake he to me, saying, Thus saith the LORD, I have anointed thee King over Israel.

And they hasted, and took every man his garment, and put it under him on the top of the stairs, and blew with trumpets, saying, Jehu is King.

So Jehu the son of Jehoshaphat the son of Nimshi conspired against Joram.

And Jehu said, If it be your minds, then let none go forth nor escape out of the City to go to tell it in Jezreel.

So Jehu rode in a Chariot, and went to Jezreel : for Joram lay there.

And there stood a Watchman on the Tower in Jezreel, and he spied the Company of Jehu as he came, and said, I see a Company. And Joram said, Take an Horseman and send to meet them, and let him say, Is it Peace ?

So there went one on horseback to meet him, and said, Thus saith the King, Is it Peace ?

And Jehu said, What hast thou to do with Peace ? Turn thee behind me.

And the Watchman told, saying, The messenger came to them, but he cometh not again.

Then he sent out a second on horseback, which came to them and said, Thus saith the King, Is it Peace ? And Jehu answered, What hast thou to do with Peace ? Turn thee behind me.

And the Watchman told, saying, He came even unto them, and cometh not again : and the driving is like the driving of Jehu the son of Nimshi ; for he driveth furiously.

And Joram said, Make ready. And his Chariot was made ready. And Joram King of Israel and Ahaziah King of Judah went out, each in his Chariot, and they went out against Jehu, and met him in the Portion of Naboth the Jezreelite.

And it came to pass, when Joram saw Jehu, that he said, Is it Peace, Jehu? And he answered, What peace, so long as the whoredoms of thy Mother Jezebel and her witchcrafts are so many?

And Joram turned his hands, and fled, and said to Ahaziah, There is Treachery, O Ahaziah.

And Jehu drew a bow with his full strength, and smote Jehoram between his arms, and the arrow went out at his heart, and he sunk down in his Chariot.

Then said Jehu to Bidkar his Captain, Take up, and cast him in the Portion of the field of Naboth the Jezreelite : for remember how that, when I and thou rode together after Ahab his father, the LORD laid this burden upon him ;

Surely I have seen yesterday the Blood of Naboth, and the Blood of his sons, saith the LORD ; and I will requite thee in this Plat, saith the LORD.

Now therefore take and cast him into the Plat of ground, according to the word of the LORD.

And when Jehu was come to Jezreel, Jezebel heard of it ; and she painted her face, and tired her head, and looked out at a window.

And as Jehu entered in at the Gate, She said, Had Zimri Peace, who slew his Master?

And he lifted up his face to the window, and said, Who is on my side? Who? And there looked out to him two or three eunuchs.

And he said, Throw her down. So they threw her down : and some of her Blood was sprinkled on the Wall, and on the Horses : and he trode her under foot.

And when he was come in, he did eat and drink, and said, Go, see now this cursed woman, and bury her : for she is a King's Daughter.

And they went to bury her : but they found no more of her than the
Scull, and the Feet, and the Palms of her Hands.

Wherefore they came again, and told him. And he said, This is the
word of the Lord, which He spake by His servant Elijah the Tishbite,
saying,

In the Portion of Jezreel shall Dogs eat the Flesh of Jezebel.

1 Kings xxi.

2 Kings ix.

" Innumerable
Disturbances on Earth through Femal snares,

.   .   .   .

Which infinite calamitie shall cause
To Humane life, and houshold peace confound."

Paradise Lost, Ed. 1667, bk. ix. l. 896.

...when a multitude of shepherds is called forth against him, he will not be afraid ... nor abase himself for the noise of them:

XII

THE LION.

JUDAH is a Lion's Whelp : from the prey, my son, thou art gone up :

He stooped down, he couched as a Lion, and as an Old Lion : who shall rouse him up ?

GENESIS XLIX. 9.

Woe to them that go down to Egypt for help; and stay on Horses, and trust in Chariots, because they are many; and in Horsemen, because they are very strong; But they look not unto the Holy One of Israel, neither seek the LORD !

Yet He also is wise, and will bring evil, and will not call back His words : but will arise against the house of the evildoers, and against the help of them that work iniquity.

Now the Egyptians are men, and not GOD; and their Horses flesh, and not Spirit. When the LORD shall stretch out His hand, both he that helpeth shall fall, and he that is holpen shall fall down, and they all shall fall together.

For thus hath the LORD spoken unto me, Like as the Lion and the young Lion roaring on his prey, when a Multitude of Shepherds is called forth against him, he will not be afraid of their Voice, nor abase himself for the Noise of them : So shall the LORD of Hosts come down to fight for Mount Zion, and for the Hill thereof.

As birds flying, so will the LORD of Hosts defend Jerusalem; defending also He will deliver it; and passing over He will preserve it.

ISAIAH XXXI. 1-5.

Set up the standard toward Zion : retire, stay not : for I will bring evil from the North, and a great destruction.

The Lion is come up from his thicket, and the destroyer of the Gentiles is on his way : he is gone forth from his place to make thy Land desolate ; and thy Cities shall be laid waste, without an inhabitant.

For this gird you with sackcloth, lament and howl : for the fierce anger of the LORD is not turned back from us.

JEREMIAH IV. 6-8.

Yet I am the LORD thy GOD from the Land of Egypt, and thou shalt know no god but Me : for there is no saviour beside Me.

I did know thee in the Wilderness, in the Land of great Drought.

According to their pasture, so were they filled ; they were filled, and their heart was exalted ; therefore have they forgotten Me.

Therefore I will be unto them as a Lion : as a Leopard by the way will I observe them :

I will meet them as a Bear that is bereaved of her whelps, and will rend the caul of their heart, and there will I devour them like a Lion : the wild beast shall tear them :

O Israel, thou hast destroyed thyself ; but in Me is thy help.

HOSEA XIII. 4-9.

" Down from a Hill the Beast that reigns in Woods,
First Hunter then, pursu'd a gentle brace
Goodliest of all the Forrest, Hart and Hinde ;
Direct to th' Eastern Gate was bent thir flight."

Paradise Lost, Ed. 1667, bk. x. ll. 187-190.

their houses shall be full of doleful creatures

XIII

BABYLON A COURT FOR OWLS.

And Babylon, the glory of Kingdoms, the beauty of the Chaldees' excellency, shall be as when God overthrew Sodom and Gomorrah.

It shall never be inhabited, neither shall it be dwelt in from generation to generation : neither shall the Arabian pitch tent there ; neither shall the Shepherds make their fold there.

But Wild Beasts of the Desert shall lie there ; and their houses shall be full of Doleful Creatures ; and Owls shall dwell there, and Satyrs shall dance there.

And the Wild Beasts of the islands shall cry in their desolate houses, and Dragons in their pleasant palaces : and her time is near to come, and her days shall not be prolonged.

For the Lord will have mercy on Jacob, and will yet choose Israel, and set them in their own Land : and the Strangers shall be joined with them, and they shall cleave to the House of Jacob.

And the People shall take them, and bring them to their place : and the House of Israel shall possess them in the Land of the Lord for servants and handmaids : and they shall take them captives, whose captives they were ; and they shall rule over their oppressors.

And it shall come to pass in the day that the Lord shall give thee rest from thy Sorrow, and from thy Fear, and from the hard Bondage wherein thou wast made to serve, that thou shalt take up this proverb against the King of Babylon and say,

How hath the oppressor ceased! the Golden City ceased!

The LORD hath broken the Staff of the Wicked, and the Sceptre of the Rulers.

He who smote the People in Wrath with a continual Stroke, he that ruled the Nations in Anger, is persecuted, and none hindereth.

The whole Earth is at rest, and is quiet: they break forth into Singing.

Yea, the Fir-trees rejoice at thee, and the Cedars of Lebanon, saying, Since thou art laid down, no Feller is come up against us.

Hell from beneath is moved for thee to meet thee at thy coming : it stirreth up the Dead for thee, even all the Chief ones of the Earth ; it hath raised up from their Thrones all the Kings of the Nations.

All they shall speak and say unto thee, Art thou also become weak as we? Art thou become like unto us ?

Thy Pomp is brought down to the Grave, and the Noise of thy Viols : the Worm is spread under thee, and the Worms cover thee.

How art thou fallen from Heaven, O Lucifer, Son of the Morning! How art thou cut down to the ground, which didst weaken the Nations!

For thou hast said in thy heart, I will ascend into Heaven, I will exalt my throne above the Stars of GOD : I will sit also upon the Mount of the Congregation, in the sides of the North :

I will ascend above the heights of the Clouds; I will be like the Most High.

Yet thou shalt be brought down to Hell, to the sides of the Pit.

They that see thee shall narrowly look upon thee, and consider thee, saying, Is this the man that made the Earth to tremble ? that did shake Kingdoms ? that made the World as a Wilderness, and destroyed the Cities thereof ? that opened not the House of his Prisoners ?

All the Kings of the Nations, even all of them, lie in Glory, every one in his own House.

But thou art cast out of thy Grave like an abominable Branch, and as the Raiment of those that are slain, thrust through with a Sword, that go down to the stones of the Pit; as a Carcase trodden under feet.

Thou shalt not be joined with them in Burial, because thou hast destroyed thy Land, and slain thy People. The Seed of Evildoers shall never be renowned.

Prepare slaughter for his Children for the iniquity of their Fathers; that they do not rise, nor possess the Land, nor fill the face of the World with Cities.

For I will rise up against them, saith the LORD of Hosts, and cut off from Babylon the Name, and Remnant, and Son, and Nephew, saith the LORD.

I will also make it a possession for the Bittern, and Pools of Water: and I will sweep it with the Besom of Destruction, saith the LORD of Hosts.

ISAIAH XIII. 19–XIV. 23.

The Sword of the LORD is filled with Blood, it is made fat with fatness, and with the blood of lambs and goats, with the fat of the kidneys of rams: for the LORD hath a sacrifice in Bosrah, and a great slaughter in the Land of Idumea.

And the Unicorns shall come down with them, and the Bullocks with the Bulls; and their Land shall be soaked with blood, and their dust made fat with fatness.

For it is the day of the LORD's Vengeance, and the year of Recompences for the Controversy of Zion.

And the Streams thereof shall be turned into Pitch, and the Dust thereof into Brimstone, and the Land thereof shall become burning Pitch.

It shall not be quenched night nor day; the Smoke thereof shall go up for ever: from generation to generation it shall lie waste; none shall pass through it for ever and ever.

But the Cormorant and the Bittern shall possess it : the Owl also and the
Raven shall dwell in it : and He shall stretch out upon it the line of
Confusion, and the Stones of Emptiness.

They shall call the Nobles thereof to the Kingdom, but none shall be there,
and all her Princes shall be Nothing.

And Thorns shall come up in her Palaces, Nettles and Brambles in the
Fortresses thereof : and it shall be an Habitation of Dragons, and a
Court for Owls.

The Wild Beasts of the Desert shall also meet with the Wild Beasts of the
Island, and the Satyr shall cry to his fellow ; the Screech Owl also shall
rest there, and find for herself a place of rest.

There shall the Great Owl make her nest, and lay, and hatch, and gather
under her shadow :

There shall the Vultures also be gathered, every one with her mate.

Seek ye out of the Book of the LORD, and read : no one of these shall fail,
none shall want her mate : for My mouth it hath commanded, and His
spirit it hath gathered them.

And He hath cast the lot for them, and His hand hath divided it unto them
by line : they shall possess it for ever, from generation to generation
shall they dwell therein.

ISAIAH XXXIV. 6–17.

A Sword is upon the Chaldeans, saith the LORD, and upon the Inhabitants
of Babylon, and upon her Princes, and upon her Wise Men.

A Sword is upon the Liars ; and they shall dote : A Sword is upon her Mighty
Men ; and they shall be dismayed.

A Sword is upon their Horses, and upon their Chariots, and upon all the
mingled People that are in the midst of her ; and they shall become as
Women : A Sword is upon her Treasures ; and they shall be robbed.

A Drought is upon her Waters ; and they shall be dried up : for it is the land
of Graven Images, and they are mad upon their Idols.

Therefore the Wild Beasts of the Desert with the Wild Beasts of the Islands
shall dwell there, and the Owls shall dwell therein : and it shall be no

more inhabited for ever ; neither shall it be dwelt in from generation to generation.

As God overthrew Sodom and Gomorrah and the neighbour Cities thereof, saith the Lord ; so shall no man abide there, neither shall any son of man dwell therein.

JEREMIAH L. 35-40.

Babylon the Great is fallen, is fallen, and is become the Habitation of Devils, and the Hold of every foul Spirit, and a Cage of every unclean and hateful Bird.

REVELATION XVIII. 2.

the Heavens knoweth her appointed times;
...de and the Crane, and the Swallow
...e time of their coming;
...e judgment of the Lord.

XIV.

THE STORK AND THE SWALLOW

WHY then is this People of Jerusalem slidden back by a perpetual Back-
sliding? They hold fast Deceit, they refuse to return.

I hearkened and heard, but they spake not aright : No man repented of his
wickedness, saying, What have I done?

Every one turned to his course, as the Horse rusheth into the Battle.

Yea, the Stork in the heaven knoweth her appointed times; and the Turtle
and the Crane and the Swallow observe the time of their coming; But
my People doth not know the Judgement of the LORD.

JEREMIAH VIII. 5-7.

"There the Eagle and the Stork
On Cliffs and Cedar tops thir Eyries build :
Part loosely wing the Region, part more wise
In common, rang'd in figure wedge thir way,
Intelligent of seasons, and set forth
Thir Aierie Caravan high over Seas
Flying, and over Lands with mutual wing
Easing thir flight; so stears the prudent Crane
Her annual Voiage, born on Windes; the Aire
Floats, as they pass, fann'd with unnumber'd plumes."

Paradise Lost, Ed. 1667, bk. vii. ll. 423-432.

Can the Ethiopian change his skin,
or the Leopard his spots?
then may ye also do Good, that are accustomed to do Evil.

JB

XV.

THE LEOPARD.

AND if thou say in thine heart, Wherefore come these things upon me?

For the greatness of thine iniquity are thy skirts discovered, and thy heels made bare.

Can the Ethiopian change his skin, or the Leopard his spots? Then may ye also do Good, that are accustomed to do Evil.

Therefore will I scatter them as the Stubble that passeth away by the Wind of the Wilderness.

This is thy lot, the portion of thy measures from Me, saith the LORD; because thou hast forgotten Me, and trusted in falsehood.

JEREMIAH XIII. 22–25.

And I will make Rabbah a stable for Camels,
and the Ammonites a couching place for flocks; and ye shall know that I am the LORD.

XVI

RABBAH A STABLE FOR CAMELS.

THE word of the Lord came unto me, saying,

Son of man, set thy face against the Ammonites, and prophesy against them ;

And say unto the Ammonites, Hear the word of the Lord God ; Thus saith the Lord God ; Because thou saidst, Aha, against My Sanctuary, when it was profaned ; and against the Land of Israel, when it was desolate ; and against the House of Judah, when they went into Captivity ;

Behold, therefore I will deliver thee to the men of the East for a Possession, and they shall set their Palaces in thee, and make their Dwellings in thee : they shall eat thy Fruit, and they shall drink thy Milk.

And I will make Rabbah a Stable for Camels, and the Ammonites a Couching place for Flocks : and ye shall know that I am the Lord.

For thus saith the Lord God ; Because thou hast clapped thine hands, and stamped with the feet, and rejoiced in heart with all thy despite against the Land of Israel ;

Behold, therefore I will stretch out Mine hand upon thee, and will deliver thee for a Spoil to the Heathen ; and I will cut thee off from the People, and I will cause thee to perish out of the Countries : I will destroy thee ; and thou shalt know that I am the Lord.

EZEKIEL XXV. 1-7.

"First *Moloch*, horrid King besmear'd with blood
Of human sacrifice, and parents tears,
Though for the noyse of Drums and Timbrels loud
Their childrens cries unheard, that past through fire
To his grim Idol.   Him the Ammonite
Worshipt in *Rabba* and her watry Plain,
In *Argob* and in *Basan*, to the stream
Of utmost *Arnon*.   Nor content with such
Audacious neighbourhood, the wisest heart
Of *Solomon* he led by fraud to build
His Temple right against the Temple of God
On that opprobrious Hill, and made his Grove
The pleasant Valley of *Hinnom*, *Tophet* thence
And black *Gehenna* call'd, the Type of Hell."

Paradise Lost, Ed. 1667, bk. i. ll. 392–406.

XVII

THE FOWLS OF THE AIR

BUT ask now the Beasts, and they shall teach thee; And the Fowls of the
Air, and they shall tell thee :
Or speak to the Earth, and it shall teach thee : And the Fishes of the Sea
shall declare unto thee.

JOB XII. 7, 8.

Behold the Fowls of the Air : For they sow not, neither do they reap, nor
gather into barns; Yet your Heavenly Father feedeth them. Are ye
not much better than they?

MATTHEW VI. 26.

> "Curs'd is the ground for thy sake, thou in sorrow
> Shalt eate thereof all the days of thy Life;
> Thornes also and Thistles it shall bring thee forth
> Unbid, and thou shalt eate th' Herb of th' Field,
> In the sweat of thy Face shalt thou eate Bread,
> Till thou return unto the ground, for thou
> Out of the ground wast taken, know thy Birth,
> For dust thou art, and shalt to dust returne."

Paradise Lost, Ed. 1667, bk. ix. ll. 201-208.

The whole Herd of Swine ran violently down a steep place into the sea and perished in the waters.

XVIII.

THE HERD OF SWINE.

AND they arrived at the Country of the Gadarenes, which is over against
Galilee.

And when He went forth to land, there met Him out of the City a certain
man, which had devils long time, and ware no clothes, neither abode in
any house, but in the Tombs.

When he saw Jesus, he cried out, and fell down before Him, and with a loud
voice said, What have I to do with Thee, Jesus, thou Son of GOD Most
High? I beseech Thee, torment me not.

For He had commanded the unclean spirit to come out of the man. For
oftentimes it had caught him : and he was kept bound with chains
and in fetters ; and he brake the bands, and was driven of the Devil
into the Wilderness.

And Jesus asked him, saying, What is thy Name? And he said, Legion :
because many devils were entered into him.

And they besought Him that He would not command them to go out into
the Deep.

And there was there an Herd of many Swine feeding on the mountain : and
they besought Him that He would suffer them to enter into them.
And He suffered them.

Then went the devils out of the man, and entered into the Swine : and the
Herd ran violently down a steep place into the Lake, and were choked.

When they that fed them saw what was done, they fled, and went and told
it in the City and in the Country.

THE HERD OF SWINE.

Then they went out to see what was done ; and came to Jesus, and found the
man, out of whom the devils were departed, sitting at the feet of Jesus,
clothed, and in his right mind : and they were afraid.

They also which saw it told them by what means he that was possessed
of the devils was healed.

Then the whole multitude of the Country of the Gadarenes round about
besought Him to depart from them ; for they were taken with great
fear :

And He went up into the ship, and returned back again.

Now the man out of whom the devils were departed besought Him that
he might be with Him : but Jesus sent him away, saying,

Return to thine own house, and shew how great things GOD hath done
unto thee. And he went his way, and published throughout the
whole City how great things Jesus had done unto him.

And it came to pass, that, when Jesus was returned, the people gladly
received Him : for they were all waiting for Him.

LUKE VIII. 26–40.

And the Swine, though he divide the Hoof, and be cloven-footed, yet he
cheweth not the Cud ; he is unclean to you.

Of their flesh shall ye not eat, and their carcase shall ye not touch ; they
are unclean to you.

LEVITICUS XI. 7, 8.

I have spread out My hands all the day unto a rebellious People, which
walketh in a way that was not good, after their own thoughts ;

A People that provoketh Me to anger continually to My face ; that
sacrificeth in Gardens, and burneth incense upon Altars of brick ;

Which remain among the Graves, and lodge in the Monuments, which
eat Swine's flesh, and Broth of Abominable things is in their vessels ;

Which say, Stand by thyself, come not near to me ; for I am holier than
thou. These are a smoke in My nose, a fire that burneth all the day.

ISAIAH LXV. 2–5.

50

THE HERD OF SWINE.

" Hereafter learn with awe
To dread the Son of God: He, all unarm'd,
Shall chase thee with the Terror of his Voice
From thy Demoniac holds, Possession foul,
Thee and thy Legions; yelling they shall fly
And beg to hide them in a Herd of Swine,
Lest He command them down into the Deep,
Bound, and to Torment sent before their Time.
Hail, Son of the Most High, Heir of both Worlds,
Queller of Satan!"

Paradise Regained, bk. iv. ll. 625–634.

—even as a Hen gathereth her Chickens under her wings—

JB

XIX.

THE HEN AND CHICKENS.

O JERUSALEM, Jerusalem, thou that killest the Prophets and stonest them
which are sent unto thee, how often would I have gathered thy
Children together, even as a Hen gathereth her Chickens under her
Wings, and ye would not!
Behold, your House is left unto you desolate.

MATTHEW XXIII. 37, 38.

> "The rest shall hear me call, and oft be warnd
> Thir sinful state, and to appease betimes
> Th' incensed Deitie, while offerd grace
> Invites; for I will cleer thir senses dark,
> What may suffice, and soft'n stonie hearts
> To pray, repent, and bring obedience due.
> To prayer, repentance, and obedience due,
> Though but endeavord with sincere intent,
> Mine eare shall not be slow, mine eye not shut.
> And I will place within them as a guide
> My Umpire *Conscience*, whom if they will hear,
> Light after light well us'd they shall attain,
> And to the end persisting, safe arrive.
> This my long sufferance and my day of grace
> They who neglect and scorn, shall never taste;
> But hard be hard'nd, blind be blinded more,
> That they may stumble on, and deeper fall;
> And none but such from mercy I exclude."

Paradise Lost, Ed. 1667, bk. iii. ll. 185-202.

The Dogs came and licked his sores

XX

LAZARUS.

THERE was a certain Rich man, which was clothed in Purple and fine
Linen, and fared sumptuously every day :

And there was a certain Beggar named Lazarus, which was laid at his
Gate, full of sores,

And desiring to be fed with the Crumbs which fell from the Rich man's
table :

Moreover the Dogs came and licked his sores.

And it came to pass that the Beggar died, and was carried by the Angels
into Abraham's bosom :

The Rich man also died, and was buried ; and in Hell he lift up his
eyes, being in torments, and seeth Abraham afar off, and Lazarus
in his bosom.

And he cried and said, Father Abraham, have mercy on me, and send
Lazarus, that he may dip the tip of his finger in water, and cool
my tongue ; for I am tormented in this flame.

But Abraham said, Son, Remember that thou in thy lifetime receivedst
thy good things, and likewise Lazarus evil things : but now he is
comforted, and thou art tormented.

And beside all this, between us and you there is a great Gulf fixed :
so that they which would pass from hence to you cannot; neither
can they pass to us, that would come from thence.

Then he said, I pray thee therefore, Father, that thou wouldest send him to my father's house :

For I have five brethren ; that he may testify unto them, lest they also come into this Place of Torment.

Abraham saith unto him, They have Moses and the Prophets ; let them hear them.

And he said, Nay, Father Abraham : but if one went unto them from the Dead, they will repent.

And he said unto him, If they hear not Moses and the Prophets, neither will they be persuaded, though one rose from the Dead.

LUKE XVI. 19-31.

...and when Paul had gathered a bundle of Sticks and laid them on the fire there came a viper out of the heat and fastened on his hand...

And when the Barbarians saw the venomous beast hang on his hand they said among themselves...

No doubt this Man is a murderer ... though he hath escaped the Sea yet Vengeance suffereth not to live.

... shook off the beast into the fire and felt no harm.

XXI

THE VIPER.

AND when they were escaped, then they knew that the Island was called
Melita.

And the Barbarous people shewed us no little kindness : for they kindled
a Fire, and received us every one, because of the present rain, and
because of the cold.

And when Paul had gathered a bundle of sticks, and laid them on the
Fire, there came a Viper out of the heat, and fastened on his hand.

And when the Barbarians saw the Venomous Beast hang on his hand,
they said among themselves, No doubt this man is a Murderer, whom,
though he hath escaped the Sea, yet Vengeance suffereth not to live.

And he shook off the Beast into the Fire, and felt no harm.

Howbeit they looked when he should have swollen, or fallen down dead
suddenly : but after they had looked a great while, and saw no harm
come to him, they changed their minds, and said that he was a God.

ACTS XXVIII. 1–6.

And these signs shall follow them that believe ; In My name shall they
cast out devils ; they shall speak with new tongues ;

They shall take up Serpents ; and if they drink any deadly thing, it shall
not hurt them ; they shall lay hands on the sick, and they shall
recover.

MARK XVI. 17, 18.

...in the Horses' mouths, that they may obey us; and we turn about their whole body. Behold also the Ships, which, though they be so great, and are driven of fierce winds, yet are they turned about with a very small helm, whithersoever the Governor listeth. Even so the Tongue is a little member, and boasteth great things.

XXII

HORSES AND SHIPS.

BEHOLD, we put Bits in the Horses' mouths, that they may obey us; and we turn about their whole Body.

Behold also the Ships, which though they be so great, and are driven of fierce winds, yet are they turned about with a very small Helm, whithersoever the Governor listeth.

Even so the Tongue is a little member, and boasteth great things.

Behold, how great a matter a little fire kindleth!

JAMES III. 3–5.

> " On th' other side uprose
> *Belial*, in act more graceful and humane;
> A fairer person lost not Heav'n; he seemed
> For dignity compos'd and high exploit:
> But all was false and hollow; though his Tongue
> Dropt Manna, and could make the worse appear
> The better reason, to perplex and dash
> Maturest Counsels: for his thoughts were low;
> To vice industrious, but to Nobler deeds
> Timorous and slothful: yet he pleas'd the ear."
>
> *Paradise Lost*, Ed. 1667, bk. ii. ll. 108–117.

www.ingramcontent.com/pod-product-compliance
Lightning Source LLC
Chambersburg PA
CBHW030554270326
41927CB00007B/908